Noah's Ark
and Other Bible Stories

Look and Find®

pi kids

publications international, ltd.

God made Adam and Eve, and gave them a true paradise in which to live — the Garden of Eden. But God wanted to test them, so he told them not to eat from a forbidden tree. Do you see that apple tree? Can you find these other trees, too?

BANANA TREE

LIME TREE

KIWI TREE

ORANGE TREE

PEAR TREE

PINEAPPLE TREES

God sent a great flood to wipe the world clean. But Noah was a good man, so God saved him. Noah and his family built a big boat called an ark and filled it with two of every animal. Can you find these animal pairs getting ready to sail?

COUGARS

MONARCH BUTTERFLIES

ANTELOPES

TURKEYS

PYTHONS

SNAILS

FOXES

ANTEATERS

Joseph's father gave him a beautiful colored coat. This made Joseph's brothers jealous. They took Joseph's coat and sold him into slavery. Search the traveling marketplace for Joseph's sneaky siblings.

REUBEN

DAN & NAPHTALI

ISSACHAR & ZEBULUN

JUDAH

GAD & ASHER

SIMEON & LEVI

BENJAMIN

The people of Israel were the slaves of Pharaoh, the Egyptian king. God sent Moses to free them. When Pharaoh didn't obey, God sent 10 plagues to change his mind. While a plague of frogs hops across the desert, look for these fancy Egyptian items.

SCARAB

SARCOPHAGUS

HIEROGLYPHIC WRITING

MAGICIAN'S STAFF

EGYPTIAN CAT

SPHINX

GOLDEN CROCODILE

PAPYRUS SCROLL

Free at last! With Pharaoh's army in hot pursuit, Moses parted the Red Sea. The Israelites made it across, while Pharaoh's army didn't. Search the crowd for these people running from the Egyptians.

GIRL AND HER DOG

MOSES

MOTHER AND BABY

MAN ON CRUTCHES

MAGICIAN

RABBI

CHARIOT DRIVER

As a shepherd boy, it was David's job to protect the flock. If a predator tried to steal a sheep, David and his sling stopped them. Each day David sat in the pasture and played music to God. Look for David's harp, as well as these other Biblical musical instruments.

PIPE

TAMBOURINE

CASTANETS

ZITHER

LUTE

HARP

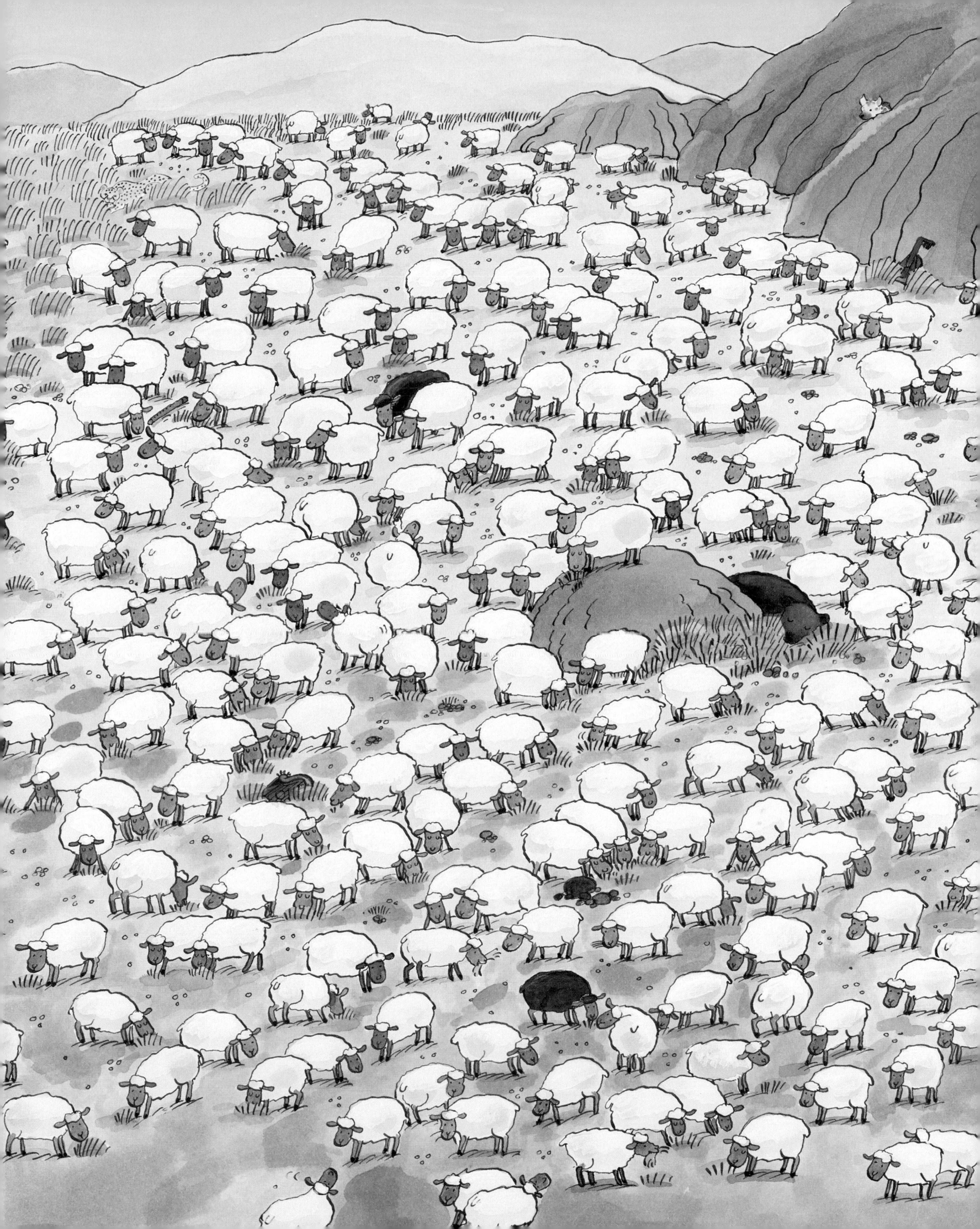

The Israelites were scared of Goliath, a giant who fought for the Philistines. But David wasn't afraid. He defeated Goliath with only a small stone, his sling, and God's help. Search the battlefield for this battle gear the small shepherd boy didn't need.

A SPEAR

A CHAIN-MAIL HELMET

A BOW AND ARROW

A SHIELD

A HELMET WITH A FEATHER

A SWORD

Jonah didn't listen to God. So God sent a whale to swallow Jonah up. The whale kept Jonah in its belly for three days and nights until the man decided to obey God. Look for these things Jonah saw while he waited.

Scroll

Sandal

Bag of gold

Pot

Sail

Fishing net

Return to the Garden of Eden and find these cute and cuddly animals that kept Adam and Eve company.

CHIMPANZEE

RABBIT

KOALA

SLOTH

PANDA

HEDGEHOG

RACCOON

BUSHBABY

PLATYPUS

Paddle back to the ark and look for these things that will help Noah get ready for the flood.

HAMMER

DOVE IN CAGE

BUCKET OF TAR

AXE

ARK BLUEPRINTS

SAW

CUBIT RULER

Go back to the scene where Joseph is sold into slavery and look for these colorful items that will remind him of his special coat.

ORANGE FLAG

RED TURBAN

YELLOW LEMON

GREEN CACTUS

BLUE SAPPHIRE

PURPLE VEIL

Ride your chariot back to Pharaoh's kingdom and find 50 frogs that God sent as a plague over Egypt.

Cross the Red Sea again and look for these ocean animals hiding in the walls of water.

STARFISH

HAMMERHEAD SHARK

JELLYFISH

EEL

STINGRAY

PUFFERFISH

Prowl back to David's flock of sheep and find these wily predators looking for a lamb chop.

EAGLE

CHEETAH

LION

WOLF IN SHEEP'S CLOTHING

BEAR

HYENA

Slingshot back to the battle between David and Goliath and look for these Israelite soldiers who are terrified of the Philistine giant.

Paddle back to Jonah and the whale and look for these modern things that seem to be a bit out of place.

LIFE VEST

JNH 117

LICENSE PLATE

SURFBOARD

VOLLEYBALL

FISHING ROD

TIN CAN

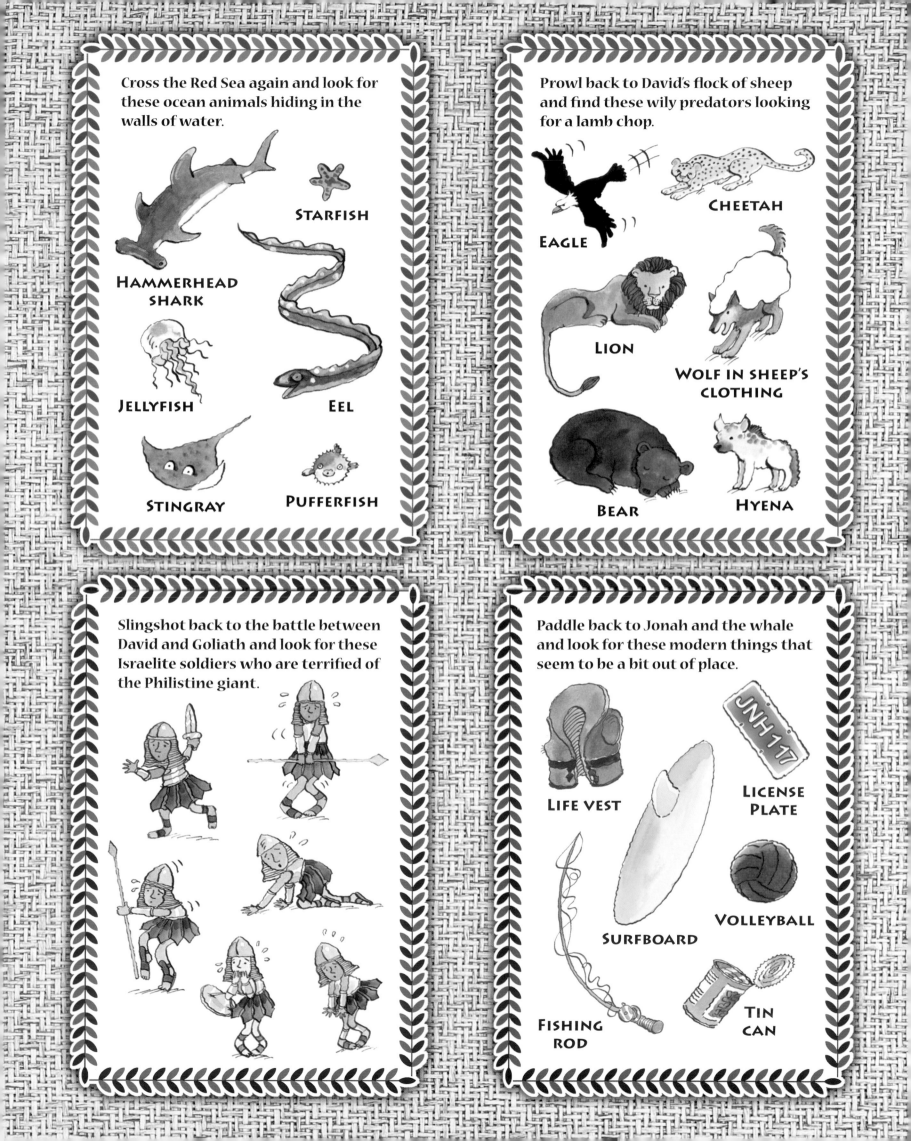